MAGISTERIAL AUTHORITY

by

Father Chad Ripperger, PhD

Reprint from
Christian Order
February-April, 2014.

Table of Contents

I: PAPAL INFALLIBILITY   4
    1. Immediate Principles   4
    2. Popes Who have Committed Error While
       Pope   9
    3. Qualities of Infallible Statements   12

II: VARIOUS ORGANS OF INFALLIBILITY   15
    1. When is the Pope Infallible?   16
    2. When Are the Bishops Infallible?   18
    3. Solemn Condemnations   26
    4. *De Fide non Definita*   27
       A. Patristics   28
       B. Theologians   30
       C. *Sensus Fidelium* or Passive
          Infallibility   31
       D. The Assent Due to Non-infallible
          Statements of the Church 32
    Synesis   39
    Gnome   41

III: PRINCIPLES OF JUDGMENT   46
    A. Natural Principles   47
    B. Supernatural Principles   48

IV: THE PROPER RESPONSE TO AN ERRING
    MAGISTERIAL MEMBER   53

Within the confines of theological discussions among the various members of the Church, the conclusions arrived at are often diametrically opposed between the different camps and, in some cases, even within the same ideological camps. Aside from a general collapse in intellectual precision, theological and philosophical principles, as well as basic logic, the members of the Church will not climb out of this tumultuous period without two things being achieved.[1]

The first is to reverse the practice since the Second Vatican Council onward not to police the doctrinal integrity among the bishops, priest, theologians, et. al. The Roman Catholic Church is a top-down governed society, not a bottom-up; this is, of course, by divine institution itself. In effect, it is

---

[1]Here we prescind from the spiritual requirements necessary to end this period of ecclesial decline.

the role of the shepherd to tell the sheep where to eat, not the sheep to tell the shepherd. Until the shepherds reassert the doctrinal authority inherent, above all, in the papacy as well as in the episcopacy, doctrinal, moral and disciplinary confusion will reign unabated.

The second is that the members of the Church, particularly the theologians, must put aside the intellectual haze of Modernist thinking, ground themselves in realist philosophy and theology and submit to the teachings of the Church in the manner, understanding and degree of certitude by which the Church asserts those teachings. This would require many of them to put aside their pontificating (including the posturing of many of them in such a way as to imply their own "infallibility") and have the intellectual humility to be willing to submit to the reality of Catholic truth and forego the mindset that they constitute a parallel Magisterium. Salvation comes from God and the terms of that salvation are entirely upon God's terms. As we approach God, therefore, we must submit to Him and those who He has placed as custodians of the mysteries of God [I Cor. 4:1].

The purpose of this article is to provide some clarity about the nature of magisterial teaching, the degrees of certitude regarding various teachings as well as clarity about what the nature of promulgation of Church teachings tells about what the Church is NOT teaching. If precision is obtained in relation to the nature of the various teachings and their degree of certitude, much of the confusion and bitterness of disagreements among members of the Church can be avoided. This article will address, in the process of laying out the theological principles, how one is to approach theological statements by various members of the Magisterium that contradict other members of the Magisterium.

I: PAPAL INFALLIBILITY

1. Immediate Principles

By divine institution[2] and by infallible proclamation, the Roman Catholic Church teaches that the pope, under certain conditions, is not able to err in the proclamation of some doctrinal or moral judgment. Vatican I lays out the conditions:

> Therefore, faithfully adhering to the tradition received from the beginning of the Christian faith, to the glory of God our saviour, for the exaltation of the catholic religion and for the salvation of the Christian people, with the

---

[2]The Scriptural foundation for papal infallibility is found principally in: Matthew 16:18; Matthew 28:18-20; John 14, 15, and 16; I Timothy 3:14-15 and Acts 15:28 sq.

approval of the sacred council, we teach and define as a divinely revealed dogma that when the Roman Pontiff speaks *ex cathedra*, that is, when, 1. in the exercise of his office as shepherd and teacher of all Christians, 2. in virtue of his supreme apostolic authority, 3. he defines a doctrine concerning faith or morals to be held by the whole Church, he possesses, by the divine assistance promised to him in blessed Peter, that infallibility which the divine Redeemer willed his Church to enjoy in defining doctrine concerning faith or morals. Therefore, such definitions of the Roman pontiff are of themselves, and not by the consent of the Church, irreformable.

The First Vatican Council essentially states that *under certain conditions* and *only under those conditions* are we assured that the statements being made by a pope are infallible. Outside of these conditions for infallibility, we do NOT have the same degree of certitude about the truth of the judgement of a pope. There are members of the Church who treat ALL papal statements with the same degree of certitude: infallible. Aside from real questions of prudence, treating all papal statements as if they are infallible is NOT the mind of the Church. To do so is proximate to heresy because it rejects the precise formulation of the conditions of infallibility as laid out by Vatican I (and later Vatican II in regard to ecumenical councils) by essentially saying that the pope is infallible regardless of conditions.

among churches & religious.

Here a clear distinction must be observed between a judgment being true and a judgment being infallible. A true statement is one which adheres to reality[3] and in the case of a theological judgment, the judgment or statement adheres to what is revealed by God Who is Truth Itself. An infallible statement is also a true statement but which also contains the notion of the statement having *certitude* in that the statement cannot contain error. This is an important distinction which will be discussed much later with respect to papal statements that do not enjoy infallibility since it is possible for a pope to make a true doctrinal statement when not employing infallibility.[4] The point here is that one simply cannot dismiss a papal statement out of hand if it is not infallible but must proceed by other theological principles than those laid down by Vatican I.

To return to the conditions laid out, Vatican I has essentially said that there are three conditions for papal infallibility:

• the first condition is: *in the exercise of his office as shepherd and teacher of all Christians;* essentially

---

[3]De Ver., q.1, a. 1 (adaequatio intellectus et rei); ST I, q. 16, a. 1; SCG I, c. 59, n. 2; De Pot., q, 3, a. 17, ad 27; De anima, q. 3, ad 1 and Super Ad Tim. I, c. 6, l. 1.

[4]The principles that govern our assent to statements made by the pope when they do not enjoy infallibility will be discussed later.

an established custom
有效的

means that the pope when making a declaration must be speaking so as the supreme head of the Church. By supreme we mean that he is doing by virtue of his teaching office as pope and not as a private theologian. Here the Council is making a distinction between when the pope speaks by virtue of his office and when he does not. In the past, popes were not wont to make theological statements which would be published in any manner that did not in some way flow from the office of pope. For example, popes in the past simply did not give "private" interviews speaking as theologians because such activities too readily confuse the faithful who are not able to make the proper theological distinctions.

belief

• The second condition is also very important to understand precisely: *"in virtue of his supreme apostolic authority"* indicates that there are differing levels of papal magisterial acts. In other words, it has to be clear that he is not merely invoking his right to preach the doctrine of Christ such as in a general audience or even in an encyclical. Rather, it must be clear that he is employing his supreme apostolic authority. Why "apostolic" authority? In an infallible statement, the pope is using the authority that comes directly from Christ to St. Peter and his successors and it does not refer to some other kind of authority that may or may not be apostolic. For example, the pope may be given the "keys to the city" which do not refer to the keys of Peter but merely some honour given in a particular town when he visits. This example may appear mundane but it is important to note that there are differing levels of

concerned with the world.

7

a letter from the pope sent to all Roman Catholic bishops throughout the world.

be relevant to.

authority and in an infallible statement it must be something that pertains to his office as pope (i.e. "Apostolic") and it must also pertain to the highest level of teaching as such.

•The third condition contains two essential elements: *"he defines a doctrine concerning faith or morals to be held by the whole Church."* The first essential element is that it is something pertaining to faith and morals. If the pope makes statements about atomic physics, he could hardly be claiming to be speaking *ex cathedra*, i.e. by virtue of his office. He must also be *"defining"* the doctrinal or moral teaching; essentially, this means that he must be clarifying the doctrinal or moral teaching in such a manner to put an end to all discussion to the contrary, rendering the teaching irreformable and rendering the judgment to be "without error," i.e. he is precluding any possibility of error. If the pope makes a statement without defining it, it does not enjoy infallibility. In fact, if any one of the conditions laid out by Vatican I are lacking, the teaching is rendered non-infallible. It does not mean it is not true necessarily, but that our certitude about it is not at the same level as it is for that which is taught infallibly.

The second essential element in the above statement is that it is a teaching *"to be held by the whole Church."* Infallible statements are not intended to bind only the Latin Church or part of the Eastern Church but the WHOLE Church. This reason, along with the intention to define, precludes disciplinary matters from enjoying infallibility, such

making impossible, especially beforehand

as canon law and the like. It does not mean that at times canon law does not contain some kind of infallible statement, but if it does so, it is from some prior infallible teaching. When the pope defines a doctrine, it is his intention "to demand internal assent from all the faithful to his teaching under pain of incurring spiritual shipwreck (*naufragium fidei*) according to the expression used by Pius IX in defining the Immaculate Conception of the Blessed Virgin."[5]

agree

Why did Vatican I put conditions on papal infallibility in the first place? The reasons are twofold:

(1)the nature of the papal office is such that its teaching authority occurs on different levels or grades depending on the issue and the Church is informing the faithful that infallibility pertains to the highest aspect of the office.

(2) Historical incidences required a precise formulation because some popes had fallen into error while they were popes.

2. Popes Who have Committed Error While Pope

Pope Honorius I actually taught the Monothelite heresy in his two letters to Sergius. He was even condemned as a heretic by the Sixth

---

[5] *The Catholic Encyclopedia* (The Gilmary Society. New York. 1929. Henceforth OCE) under Infallibility.

Ecumenical Council, the decrees of which were approved by Leo II. Martin I, along with the Third Council of Constantinople, condemned the Monothelitism of Pope Honorius I.[6] Also, there is the example of the condemnation of Nicholas I who held that aside from the Trinitarian formula one could simply baptize *"in nomine Christi."*[7] Sometimes popes disagree on particular issues such as was the case with Pope Celestine III and Pope Innocent III who disagreed over issues pertaining to the Pauline privilege.[8] There is also the historical case of Pope John XXII:

> In the last years of John's pontificate there arose a dogmatic conflict about the Beatific Vision, which was brought on by himself, and which his enemies made use of to discredit him. Before his elevation to the Holy See, he had written a work on this question, in which he stated that the souls of the blessed departed do not see God until after the Last Judgment. After becoming pope, he advanced the same teaching in his sermons. In this he met with strong opposition, many theologians, who adhered to the usual opinion that the blessed departed

---

[6]Denz. 487f/251f, 496-498/253, 518/271 and 550.

[7]Denz. 646/229.

[8] Denz. 768/405.

did see God before the Resurrection of the Body and the Last Judgment, even calling his view heretical. A great commotion was aroused in the University of Paris when the General of the Minorites and a Dominican tried to disseminate there the pope's view. ...In December, 1333, the theologians at Paris, after a consultation on the question, decided in favour of the doctrine that the souls of the blessed departed saw God immediately after death or after their complete purification; at the same time they pointed out that the pope had given no decision on this question but only advanced his personal opinion, and now petitioned the pope to confirm their decision. John appointed a commission at Avignon to study the writings of the Fathers, and to discuss further the disputed question. In a consistory held on 3 January, 1334, the pope explicitly declared that he had never meant to teach contrary to Holy Scripture or the rule of faith and in fact had not intended to give any decision whatever. Before his death he withdrew his former opinion, and declared his belief that souls separated from their bodies enjoyed in heaven the Beatific Vision.[9]

---

[9]OCE, vol. VIII, p. 433ff under the entry "John XXII." As to why the case of John XXII is so important regarding tradition, see the author's book entitled *The Binding Force of Tradition* [Sensus Traditionis Press, 2013].

The case of John XXII shows why the conditions of Vatican I are so important. John XXII had made erroneous statements during "magisterial" acts, i.e. preaching. However, these acts did not meet the conditions for infallibility and so there was no guarantee that they would be infallible, i.e. they are non-infallible statements. In all of this, we recognize that God, i.e. the Holy Spirit, will ensure the pope does not fall into error when he meets those conditions. The fact that these conditions are even seen playing themselves out with St. Peter over the issue of circumcision is a sign that God, Who is the Author of Scripture, wants to affirm that while Peter and his successors are infallible, they are so only under certain conditions.

declare solemnly

3. Qualities of Infallible Statements

When we consider infallible statements of any kind, but especially in light of the formulation of Vatican I, we realize that infallible statements enjoy certain qualities.

(1) An infallible statement is NOT subject to revision by anyone, i.e. no one can change the teaching. This is extremely important because it tells us that even subsequent popes are bound by the infallible judgment.

(2) No one may lawfully pass judgment upon an infallible teaching, again, even subsequent popes or ecumenical councils.

(3) Those who maintain that it is lawful to appeal from the judgments of the Roman Pontiff "stray from the genuine path of truth."[10] In effect, any person who denies an infallible statement cannot claim to be Catholic.

(4) Infallible statements are irreformable, i.e. they are not subject to reformulation, change, alteration, etc. in regards to the understanding that was had in the intention, expressions and words of the original formula.

(5) Infallible statements give us the greatest certitude regarding the matter of our faith.

(6) Infallible definitions close the discussion on any topic falling within the infallible authority of the pope or ecumenical councils.

(7) Further development of a doctrine is possible but ONLY within the confines of the original understanding of the infallible judgment. 不可改变

(8) Infallible statements are final and irrevocable, i.e. a later pope and council CANNOT change them.

Due to the fact that the Church has been so clear about the nature of infallible statements and the conditions under which they are given, if a pope speaks in a non-infallible manner and does lapse into error, it is not grounds for scandal. In other words, aside from the fact that taking scandal itself is a sin, the fact is that it should not impact our faith in anyway if a pope were to say something contrary to

---

a mistake
resulting
from
inattention
失误

an infallible statement. Worse still, those who were to follow a pope who was in error in a non-infallible teaching which is taught contrary to something that is infallible is not, therefore, excused.

released.

II: VARIOUS ORGANS OF INFALLIBILITY

When considering the various organs or agents within the Church in which infallibility is found, we realise that the Magisterium has given a much broader understanding to it than most Catholics understand. We have already seen that the pope is infallible but we have yet to discuss fully "when" he is infallible. We also know that ecumenical councils are infallible but it will be good to discuss the conditions under which they are infallible, since it is a common misunderstanding that ecumenical councils are "always" infallible. Furthermore, popes have pointed to other organs of infallibility than the popes and councils so those will need to be addressed as well.

1. When is the Pope Infallible?

The conditions under which papal infallibility is employed is clear, as we saw in Part I. However, the question remains: when are those conditions observed in papal judgments or statements? *— term*

First, we see it when the pope issues an apostolic constitution in which the terminology is employed to indicate infallibility: as in *Ineffabilis Deus* of Pius IX defining the Immaculate Conception, or *Munificentissimus Deus* of Pius XII defining the Assumption of the Blessed Virgin Mary. In other words, the pope is found to employ infallibility when the nature of the document and its formulation clearly indicate so.

However, the pope may also be infallible outside these kinds of definitions. If one reviews the conditions of Vatican I, it did not say the pope is infallible ONLY when he is defining a positive doctrine or moral of the Church in a specific kind of document. Rather, Vatican I merely lays out the conditions which can find themselves in different kinds of papal judgments. Theologians commonly hold that the pope is infallible in two other instances. The first is canonisations of saints: *examples*

> It is also commonly and rightly held that the Church is infallible in the canonisation of saints, that is to say, when canonisation takes place according to the solemn process that has been followed since the ninth century. Mere beatification, however, as distinguished

clearly defined
決定性

from canonisation, is not held to be infallible, and in canonisation itself the only fact that is infallibly determined is that the soul of the canonised saint departed in the state of grace and already enjoys the beatific vision.[11]

This quote is loaded and needs unpacking.

First, it is commonly held by theologians that the canonisation of saints is infallible. Second, beatifications are not.[12] Third, infallibility regarding canonisation is restricted to two things: 1. that the soul departed in a state of grace; 2. that it already enjoys the beatific vision. *holy*

It is not a definitive judgment on his sanctity; it amounts directly to no more than a permission to pay him a cultus. When the Church grants this practical permission, she is, in the view of the best theologians, infallible, *"errare practice non potest."*[13] Canonisations mean the person made it to heaven. It does NOT mean that they lived heroic Christian

---

[11] *Original Catholic Encyclopedia* (OCE), Infallibility. For other theologians who discuss the infallibility of canonisations, see Ludovico Billot, *Tractatus de ecclesia Christi*, (Romae apud Aedes Universitatis Gregorianae, 1927), pp. 423- 429.

[12] This would explain Pope Benedict XVI's return to having a cardinal preside over beatifications while the pope only presides over canonisations to make the clear distinction between what is and what is not infallible.

[13] Charles Journet, *The Church of the Word Incarnate* (Sheed and Ward, London and New York, 1955), p. 348.

virtue in this life, necessarily, although in many cases it does. This should be kept in mind to avoid scandal in relation to canonising people for political reasons, ideological reasons, etc. Regardless of the human reasons, the papal magisterial act of canonisation infallibly guarantees the person is in heaven and we can have public cult in relation to that person.[14] For this reason, canonisation should not be viewed as a stamp of approval of everything the person taught or did.

2. When Are the Bishops Infallible?

Ludwig Ott observes that:

> The totality of the Bishops is infallible, when they, either assembled in general council or scattered over the earth, propose a teaching of faith or morals as one to be held by all the faithful. (De fide).[15]

He goes on to observe that this active infallibility of the bishops is assured to the incumbents of the Church's teaching office. Ott includes both the

---

[14]It is an unfortunate fact that the rigor of the canonisation process has been reduced since the Second Vatican Council. The Church needs rigor in the process to avoid it being used for bad intentions as well as to ensure the good example of those canonised as leading lives of heroic Christian virtue.

[15]Ludwig Ott, *Fundamentals of Catholic Dogma* (Tan Books. Rockford, Illinois. 1974), p. 299.

extraordinary magisterial acts of the bishops in an ecumenical council and the ordinary magisterial acts of the bishops when agreeing on a particular teaching of faith and morals. This distinction is reiterated by Vatican II and we actually see the conditions laid out for when infallibility occurs in a council:

> Although the individual bishops do not enjoy the prerogative of infallibility, they nevertheless proclaim Christ's doctrine infallibly whenever, even though dispersed through the world, but still maintaining the bond of communion among themselves and with the successor of Peter, and authentically teaching matters of faith and morals, they are in agreement on one position as definitively to be held. This is even more clearly verified when, gathered together in an ecumenical council, they are teachers and judges of faith and morals for the universal Church, whose definitions must be adhered to with the submission of faith.[16]

Each individual bishop does not of his own enjoy infallibility. This is in contrast to the pope, who by virtue of his office and when meeting the conditions we have laid out, definitively teaches on a matter of faith and morals, has no possibility of error in his

---

[16]*Lumen Gentium*, para. 25.

teaching. An individual bishop, on the other hand, does not enjoy that ability by virtue of his office.

The conditions for infallibility of the bishops, ~~summoned~~ assembled then, are the following:

Firstly, that they teach infallibly when teaching in an ecumenical council that is in union with the Roman Pontiff. If a council is convened and the Roman Pontiff does not give consent to the teachings proposed, they do not enjoy infallibility. This is why some theologians have rightly pointed out that even when the bishops are teaching throughout the world and meet ordinary magisterial infallibility requirements or when they are teaching infallibly in an ecumenical council, ultimately, these acts are infallible due to the fact that the pope consents.[17] If there was a lack of union with the pope in a council or if the bishops throughout the world began teaching something contrary to the Faith as defined or taught by the Holy Father, they

---

[17]Sylvester Berry, *The Church of Christ: an Apologetic and Dogmatic Treatise*, (Mount St. Mary's Seminary, Emmitsburg, Maryland, 1955) on page 260 observes: "Again, since the bishops enjoy infallibility in their corporate capacity only, they cannot exercise it independently of the Roman Pontiff, their divinely constituted head. From this it also follows that all definitions must have the approval and confirmation of the Roman Pontiff, for without such confirmation the bishops are acting independently of their head and, therefore, without any authority."

would not be speaking infallibly.[18]

In addition, it must include virtually all of the bishops.

> The council must be truly ecumenical by celebration, i.e., the whole body of bishops must be represented. This, of course, does not require the presence of each and every bishop of the whole Church, for if such were the case, the willful or enforced absence of one bishop would frustrate the will of the entire body. Neither is it necessary that every bishop present should consent to the definition proposed, for since the bishops individually are fallible, false opinions will almost invariably find some supporters among them. On this account it would be practically impossible to define any doctrine if unanimous consent were necessary, yet at times a definition is imperative, because some fundamental doctrine of Christianity is at stake, as happened during the Arian and Nestorian heresies. Hence a lawful and infallible definition may be made without the unanimous consent of the Fathers present. In case of a real division in a council, truth must

required
necessary.

----

[18]*Ibid.*, p. 260: "Definitions of faith may also be made by councils that are not truly ecumenical in their celebration, but in that case the infallible authority is not that of the bishops, but that of the Roman Pontiff, who approves the decrees and thus makes them his own."

acting together

21

lie with the party whom the Roman Pontiff
supports, since no definitions have any force
unless confirmed by him.[19]

[handwritten annotation: branch of astronomy concerned with physical & chemical properties.]

The second condition is that it must be in an area of
faith and morals. Like papal infallibility, if a council
or the bishops throughout the world were teaching
something on astrophysics, one is not required to
give assent since it does not pertain to their teaching
office as such to talk about astrophysics.

The third and last condition is that it must be
proposed as to be held definitively. Vatican II, in this
area is simply restating what the tradition had
always held, that what a council teaches only enjoys
infallibility if the bishops and pope intend to define
something in the area of faith and morals. If they do
not intend to define a doctrine, then infallibility is
not employed. Here we are reminded of the words of
Berry:

> A large majority of the acts of councils are
> not infallible definitions, because they are not
> intended as such. "Neither the discussions
> which precede a dogmatic decree, nor the
> reasons alleged to prove and explain it, are to
> be accepted as infallibly true. Nothing but
> the actual decrees are of faith, and these only
> if they are intended as such."[20]

---

[19] 19. *Ibid.*, p. 260.

[20] Berry, *op. cit.*, p. 261.

Berry is quoting St. Robert Bellarmine and his observation is highly important for our age. Pope Paul VI confirms the reality of this understanding by the following words from his closing speech at Vatican II: "Now truly it is helpful to observe, that (although) through her Magisterium, the Church willed to define no primary extraordinary doctrine of dogmatic belief..."[21] While all prior ecumenical councils employed infallibility in various parts of their documents, the Fathers of Vatican II chose specifically NOT to *define* any doctrine or moral matter.

Several important points logically follow from this:

(1)We should not fall into the common error today that mistakenly holds that each and every aspect of the documents of an ecumenical council is infallible. This is simply not the case. Intention to define on the side of the pope or council is required for it to be infallible.

(2) Just because a particular document or part of a document of a council does not enjoy infallibility does NOT give one the latitude to simply dismiss it or believe that one is not bound by it. Paul VI even noted this right after the above line. But the binding force of what is taught under such conditions is subject to two considerations, viz. the authority by which it is taught and its congruity with **the remote**

___

[21]Paul VI, *Homilia 'Promulgazione Alcuni Documenti Conciliari'* (December 7, 1965).

rule of faith, viz. the tradition.[22] Benedict XVI took pains to observe that Vatican II and the subsequent acts must be interpreted in light of the tradition by virtue of what he called *the hermeneutic of continuity.*

(3) Outside of these conditions, the pope and the council can err. Again, it should not be presumed that they have erred unless it can be clearly demonstrated.

(4) As a matter of piety, one ought to try to reconcile teachings of various popes. This does not require us to set aside reason when statements are clearly contradictory and assert that they have continuity. Even when a pope or an ecumenical council says something contrary to the Faith, as we have observed, that does not give one the permission to reject everything that he or the council says. Each statement must stand on its own merits and be judged in light of the remote rule.

Some will assert that if we simply do not always follow the Holy Father and the ecumenical councils in everything they say, then we are no different than Protestants who follow their own judgment in matters of religion. Such an argument is hardly worth addressing. However, as it is so common today, let us invoke the Angelic Doctor, who says that ignorance of the primary rule does not

---

[22]See this author's work, *The Binding Force of Tradition.* The entire work is dedicated to how we are bound to the tradition.

suffice and so we are not allowed simply to follow a member of the Magisterium blindly or ignorantly.[23] He observes:

> And because of this, one is not to give assent to the preaching of a prelate which is contrary to the faith since in this it is discordant with the primary rule. Nor through ignorance is a subject excused from the whole: since the habit of faith causes an inclination to the contrary, since it teaches necessarily of all things that pertain to salvation.[24]

The primary rule he is referring to here is ultimately God, but God's teachings are passed on through tradition. This is why the relationship of a particular magisterial member to the remote rule (i.e. the tradition) is of key importance.[25] Essentially all of this means that under normal conditions, we as Catholic faithful have a right to expect those who teach us to be sure that what they teach does not contradict the teachings of God or the prior Magisterium. However, we must also not be naive

---

[23] III Sent., d. 25, q. 2, a. 1d, ad 3.

[24] *Ibid.*

[25] For a further discussion of the primary and secondary rules of faith, see *The Binding Force of Tradition, op. cit.*

and presume that the Magisterium never will teach anything contrary to the Faith, for our cited examples make it clear that it has happened. Moreover, we deal with it on a daily basis by simply observing the news in which bishops are contradicting clearly defined teachings of the Church.

3. Solemn Condemnations

The great theologian, Fr. Adolphe Tanquerey, observes in his work *Synopsis Theologiae Dogmaticae* that:

The Church is infallible when it observes a certain proposition under some doctrinal censure. A Doctrinal censure is defined as: "qualification, by which a proposition is known that in some way it is opposed to faith and good morals". When a doctrine is observed as heretical, it is of the faith to be the infallible Church in discerning that censure, since this is done by an exercise of the Magisterium about a *direct* object of infallibility. If truly it is known as *a heresy proximate to the faith, an error in faith or false*, it is a common and true belief that it is held by the infallible Church: for in inflicting this kind of censure, the Church bares a true definition, granted negative. Of the doctrine which is known in another way, viz. *temerious, offensive to pious ears, improbable,* etc, it is not then evident the Church to be infallible, for it does not seem to define the doctrine: but in this case, one is always held to religious assent, even internal to the judgment of the Church.[26]

Tanquerey is noting that there is a distinction between a condemnation in which the Church's infallibility is employed[27] and one in which it is not. Those in which infallibility are employed are called solemn condemnations. An example of a solemn condemnation is Canon 1 of the document *Dei Filius* which condemns the proposition that God is not the creator of things visible and invisible. What is important to note here is that it is not enough for subsequent members of the Magisterium to propose things that have already been solemnly condemned and assume that the teaching is valid simply because they propose it.

4. *De Fide non Definita*

Ordinary Magisterial infallibility has the same requirements as extraordinary infallibility in

---

[26] *Synopsis Theologiae Dogmaticae ad Mentem S. Thomae Aquinatis Hodiernis Moribus Accomodata* (Desclee et Socii, Parisiis. 1927), vol. I, p. 556 (n. 823). See also Ludovico Billot, *Tractatus de ecclesia Christi*, (Romae apud Aedes Universitatis Gregorianae, 1927) pp. 410-18 for a longer presentation of the topic and further distinctions.

[27] This may be done either by a pope or a council.

the sense that when the bishops <u>dispersed</u> throughout the world teach something regarding faith and morals, it is infallible by ordinary magisterial infallibility when the bishops hold that the particular matter is something that pertains to the Faith. It is not simply a matter of the bishops agreeing on something but that what they agree on they also hold that it is *de fide*. This tells us that there are two kinds of *de fide* doctrines, viz. *definita* and *non definita*. Just because a doctrine has not been defined by a pope or council does not mean it is not of the Faith. The fact that John Paul II observed that the non-ordination of women to the priesthood was constantly taught in the past shows us that he is observing that teaching is *de fide*; it is infallible, even though it has not been defined. We must therefore consider other organs of infallibility, even if they do not define.

A. Patristics[28]

Agius observes that "When the Fathers of the Church consent on certain doctrines, which evidently belong to the common faith of the Church – and all the faithful believe them – then, that

---

[28]The patristics or the Fathers of the Church normally refer to those who lived from after the death of the Apostles until sometime around or after 800 A.D. There are various opinions about when the patristic era ends: everything from around 604 all the way to 1153 with St. Bernard. See OCE under "Fathers of the Church."

consent of the Fathers shows the divine tradition of those doctrines. It is the same consent of the Universal Church. Consequently, the common consent of the Fathers is infallible, because the Church itself is infallible."[29]

The importance of the Fathers and their infallibility has been used and is a constant theme in various documents of the Church as we see in the Council of Orange,[30] Council of Trent[31] and Pius IX in *Gravissimas inter*,[32] among others.[33] It is often said by the popes that if the Patristics have a consensus regarding a specific doctrine, it is to be held to be of the Faith. While not everything that the Patristics say is infallible, nevertheless, the Patristics constitute a specific source of knowledge regarding those things which pertain to the Faith. The consensus of the Patristics is important because many modern forms of exegesis contradict the consensus of the Patristics regarding various parts of Scripture. But this is also true for various doctrines.

---

[29]George Agius (Boston, Stratford, 1928.), *Tradition and the Church*, p. 240.

[30]Denz. 370/173; 396/199.

[31]Denz. 1600/843a; 1692/905.

[32]Denz. 2855/1672.

[33]For a fuller listing, see Denz. *Index systematicus* under A7ad.

B. Theologians

When the term *Theologians* is used, it should not be confused with the generic (lower case) *theologians*. The term "Theologians" refers to a specific group of men, viz. those theologians of the various scholastic schools from the twelfth century until the middle of the eighteenth century (roughly during the years of 1100 to 1750).[34] Pius IX in *Tuas Libenter*[35] says that we are to hold those teachings as pertaining to the Faith not only found in the decrees of the councils but also in the universal and constant consensus of the Catholic Theologians. Here we see the two criteria for the infallibility of those things held by the Theologians, viz. that it must be (1) constant and (2) universally held by those theologians during that historical period. To put this teaching in context, Scannell observes:

> Although the assistance of the Holy Ghost is not directly promised to Theologians, nevertheless the assistance promised to the Church requires that He should prevent them as a body from falling into error; otherwise the Faithful who follow them would all be led astray. The consent of Theologians implies

---

[34]Herve, *ibid.*

[35]Denz. 2879/1683. See also Gregory IX, *Ab Aegyptiis* (Denz. 824/442); *Sixtus IV, Romani Pontificis provida* (Denz. 1407 [no corresponding old #]).

the consent of the episcopate, according to St. Augustine's dictum: "Not to resist an error is to approve of it - not to define a truth is to reject it."[36]

This organ of infallibility is important today due to the Modernist rejection of medieval theology; a common theme among various statements by ecclesiastics and sadly even members of the Magisterium in recent years.

C. *Sensus Fidelium* or Passive Infallibility

It has been a common teaching of the theologians that the sense of the faithful constitutes an organ of infallibility. The *Catechism of the Catholic Church* states that

> The whole of the faithful cannot err (*falli*) and the whole people manifest this particular property mediating the supernatural *sensus fidei* when "from the bishops to the last of the lay faithful" it exhibits its universal consent of things pertaining to faith and morals.[37]

---

[36]See Joseph Wilhelm and Thomas Scannell, *A Manual of Catholic Theology*, (London. Kegan Paul, Trench, Trübner & Co. Ltd. 1908) vol. 1, pp. 71-84.

[37]CCC, n. 92 (quoting Vatican II, *Lumen Gentium*, para. 12).

When the whole of the faithful consent to a particular doctrine, it is to be considered as pertaining to the Faith.[38]

The reason for this is the indefectibility of the Church: it is impossible that the whole of Christ's faithful would fall into error. While individuals, whole provinces and even nations may fall away from the Faith as we see in history, nevertheless those professing the true Faith must always remain sufficient in number and in distribution throughout the world to preserve the Church truly Catholic in the unity of faith and worship.

D. The Assent Due to Non-infallible Statements of the Church

A common theme since the time of Vatican I has been the assent required of non-infallible ordinary magisterial teaching. The term that is often used is religious assent and this term was used even before Vatican II, as we shall see. *Lumen Gentium* 25 observes:

In matters of faith and morals, the bishops speak in the name of Christ and the faithful are to accept their teaching and adhere to it

---

[38]Popes in the past have made use of the *sensus fidelium* in support of certain doctrines: e.g.. Pope Blessed Pius IX, *Ineffabilis Deus* (1854), and Pope Pius XII, *Munificentissimus Deus* (1950).

with a religious assent. This religious submission of mind and will must be shown in a special way to the authentic Magisterium of the Roman Pontiff, even when he is not speaking *ex cathedra*; that is, it must be shown in such a way that his supreme Magisterium is acknowledged with reverence, the judgments made by him are sincerely adhered to, according to his manifest mind and will. His mind and will in the matter may be known either from the character of the documents, from his frequent repetition of the same doctrine, or from his manner of speaking.

In this quote, there are several things of importance. The first is that we are not to treat everything the Holy Father says as if it is infallible. This also applies to bishops even when speaking within a council pertaining to those matters which are taught in such a fashion that they are not being taught definitively. This indicates that outside of those matters that are infallible, whether they are *de fide definita* or *de fide non-definita*, we are not to treat them with the same degree of assent.

The paragraph above teaches that of those things that are not *de fide* we are to look at several factors which would determine how bound we are by the teaching. Those factors are:

(1) The character of the document. In this respect, an encyclical or a papal bull has greater weight than

an apostolic exhortation.

(2) From the frequent repetition of the same doctrine: here we are not talking just about the same Holy Father repeating something over and over. Rather we are talking about the totality of the Magisterium throughout time and its repetition of a particular issue. This would mean that if the popes in the past have always taught something, then it may require more than just religious assent but if it is only repeated a few times in a manner that is not such that it is clear that a pope is defining the teaching, then we should give the degree of assent based upon how often it is repeated. Hence, if several popes had said one thing and a pope comes along and in a lower magisterial document says the opposite, we would follow what the prior popes said.

(3) "His manner of speaking" refers to the way in which a pope is talking. If a pope is talking in an encyclical about a new moral issue, we would be bound more by it than if he were simply making observations about some biblical text during a papal audience. Moreover, it can refer to the type of language and vocabulary used in speaking about a particular teaching.

Since we should interpret what Vatican II says in light of tradition, we should take a look at the discussion of religious assent and what that term meant prior to the Council. Tanquerey gives a short treatment of the topic which is indicative of the pre-conciliar theological discussion:

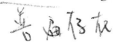

34

One is not certainly bound, therefore, to these declarations to assent of faith, but *internal* and *religious* which we establish by legitimate ecclesiastical authority; nor [is it] *absolute* assent, since the decrees are not infallible, but *prudential* and *conditioned*, so far as the presumption rests with the superior in matters of faith and morals. Some contend in this case *reverential silence suffices*, in which one remains silent in relation to those things which are declared as ~~temerious~~ or not prudent, not however, to compel *internal obedience (obsequium) of the mind* which we are held to hold in things which are entirely certain. Nevertheless, the more common belief is that one is required [to give] *internal assent* of which we treated above, then that they suggest *prudence* and *obedience* due to ecclesiastical superiors not only in disciplinary matters, but also and *a fortiori* in doctrinal matters.[39]

This short passage is very loaded and requires a great deal of parsing. The assent to those things which are not infallible must be internal and by that it means that one must submit the judgment of one's intellect and the choice of one's will to it. It is not merely a matter of external silence when one believes something entirely different. However, he

---

[39] *Synopsis Theologiae Dogmaticae*, vol. I, p. 571 (n. 844).

says that the assent is not absolute nor is it the kind of assent that one gives to a *de fide* statement, whether it is *definita* or *non-definita*.

The kind of assent one gives is based upon prudence and conditions. He uses the Latin word *conditionatus* which means that the assent that one gives is based upon an understanding that comes from the nature of what is being proposed for assent. This is why it was translated as *conditioned*. What are those conditions or how is a proposition that is proposed for assent "conditioned"?

We already saw above the observation that it is based upon how it is proposed, repetition, etc. All of this points to the degree of certitude regarding the particular doctrine and the various degrees of certitude, which are called the *theological notes*. Due to the limitations of this article, we do not have time to go into each of the various degrees of certitude,[40] but suffice it to say that the Church herself, the very mind of the Church is that we give assent to the degree of certitude of the particular doctrine being proposed. We do not treat all doctrines with the exact same level of certitude, whether they come from the pope or not. Rather, one must pay close attention to the manner in which a pope proposes it, the history and tradition of the doctrine, etc. to determine how bound one is in relationship to the particular doctrine or moral teaching. This will become very important when we begin discussing

---

[40]For a discussion of the theological notes, see *The Binding Force of Tradition, op. cit.*

what one does when one magisterial member contradicts another. In other words, what is being laid out are certain principles that must be followed when one considers the reality of various magisterial members contradicting each other.

Tanquerey also mentions that it is a matter of prudence. Here we see a key indication about the mind of the Church in how these things are to be treated. Prudence is the virtue by which one knows the right means to attain the end.[41] The end is our salvation and the means are our faith, sanctifying grace, etc. While Protestants believe in the Holy Spirit speaking to us directly regarding matters that pertain to our salvation, Catholics believe that these were made known through public Revelation. Hence we must adhere to the authority who has the right to pass judgment on the public Revelation. That authority is the Magisterium of the Church. Prudence therefore dictates that in the normal course of things, even if what is being proposed for belief is not infallible, we should normally give assent to it as a matter of prudence, i.e., to avoid entering into territory based on our own private judgment which could easily lead to our own damnation.

In other words, as a *general* rule, one should

---

[41]For a discussion of prudence, see this author's work *Introduction to the Science of Mental Health*, vol III, part II, chapter 1.

normally simply listen to the Magisterium.[42] But even the Church herself does not say that we are to do so slavishly. The fact that the Church makes a distinction between the assent that is required for infallible and non-infallible teachings indicates that the Church herself recognizes there are different degrees of certitude.

• Of those things which we have absolute certitude that pertains to them being *de fide*, we must give assent in order to be saved.

• Of those things which are not *de fide* or which we do not have absolute certitude, then there are varying degrees of certitude and therefore varying degrees of assent.

• But also there are varying circumstances which could result in a magisterial member teaching something contrary to what has been taught, that is, contrary to the remote rule of faith which is the

---

[42]That one should follow the Magisterium even in areas which are not infallible was reiterated by John Paul II in *Ad Tuendam Fidem* (1998). See also Congregation for the Doctrine of the Father, *Doctrinal Commentary on the Concluding Formula of the Professio Fidei* (1998). These two documents are important insofar as it is a sign that the teaching that one must normally submit to the teachings of the Magisterium even when they are not infallible is still part of the Church's teaching.

tradition.[43] In Part I we discussed popes who taught things that were contrary to those things which were part of the remote rule: the monothelitism of Pope Honorius I, the teaching of Pope John XXII on the disposition of people after death, etc. The very fact that Vatican I clarified the conditions of infallibility is indicative of this very reality.

So in the normal course of things one should simply follow the Magisterium. But the Church Herself recognizes by discussing the different kinds of assent that there are occasions in which a particular member or members of the Magisterium will teach things contrary to the faith. This is why St. Thomas Aquinas said we cannot follow the Magisterium blindly. When it comes to matters that are infallible or *de fide*, then we must give assent and follow blindly even if we do not see it clearly, while still having an obligation to continue to educate ourselves to understand it. When it comes to those teachings which are not infallible, we should normally follow them unless certain conditions occur which would indicate that we are not to follow them. Before we go into those conditions, a further discussion of prudence is necessary.

Synesis

There are various parts of the virtue of prudence; however, we want to focus on two of

---

[43]For a discussion of the remote rule, see *The Binding Force of Tradition, op. cit.*

them. The first is synesis,[44] a potential part[45] of prudence in which one judges those things which fall under and are according to the common law.[46] When a person contemplates a course of action, he realises that the judgment of the means falls under normal precepts. For example, if he drives off in another man's automobile he knows that it falls under the precept of "thou shalt not steal." And again, the law teaches that one ought not lie, so one can judge whether a particular act of lying falls under that common law. Synesis judges the means and not the end[47] and so by the virtue of synesis one knows when the action falls under the common law. St. Thomas notes that synesis helps one to grasp things as they are[48] and gives one a right judgment about the means.[49] For this reason, Deferrari defines synesis as "the virtue of common sense in practical

---

[44]There is no English correlating term to synesis. Most moralists simply use the term directly in English without any modification.

[45]ST II-II, q. 48, a. 1.

[46]III Sent., d. 33, q. 3, a. 1c, ad 3; ST I-II, q. 57, a. 6, ad 3; ST II-II, q. 48, a. 1; *ibid.*, q. 51, a. 4 and ibid., ad 4. See also III Sent., d. 35, q. 2, a. 4b, ad 3.

[47]ST II-II, q. 51, a. 3, ad 1.

[48]ST II-II, q. 51, a. 3, ad 1.

[49]ST I, q. 22, a. 1, ad 1. See also ST II-II, q. 60, a. 1, ad 1.

affairs, i.e., the habit of judging rightly about the practical individual cases according to the customary rules of life."[50]

梵言 Gnome

The other virtue is "gnome."[51] In ST II-II, q. 53, a. 2, St. Thomas observes that gnome is the virtue by which one judges about action when the common law does not apply or when something is not a common occurrence." In other words, this is the virtue which helps with difficult scenarios. The more this virtue is developed, the more one can act prudently in extraordinary circumstances.

To elaborate: gnome is a potential part in relation to prudence and it is the virtue which judges of those things which recede from the common law.[52] Deferrari defines it as an aptitude[53] or ability to judge rightly over the extraordinary things of

---

[50]Deferrari in *A Latin-English Dictionary of St. Thomas* (St. Paul Editions. Boston. 1986), p. 1026.

[51]Like synesis, there is no English correlating term to gnome. Most moralists simply use the term directly in English without any modification.

[52]ST I-II, q. 57, a. 6, ad 3; ST II-II, q. 51, a. 4 and ST II-II, q. 80, a. 1, ad 4. See also De Vir., q. 5, a. 1.

[53]Gnome implies a certain perspicacity of judgment, see ST II-II, q. 51, a. 4 and ibid., ad 3.

41

life."[54] Sometimes it happens to a person that the circumstances in which he finds himself are out of the ordinary and not common and so the virtue of gnome helps him to judge what to do according to "higher principles."[55] In *Prima Secundae*, St. Thomas indicates that the higher principles are the natural law itself.[56] This means that in order to exercise the virtue of gnome, a person has to have knowledge not just of general precepts, such as "thou shalt not steal," but about the very structure of human nature and the application of the natural law in concrete circumstances.

How does this apply to our current discussion on what one does if a particular magisterial member speaks things contrary to the Faith? To begin with, there are natural virtues which have man as their cause in which we can increase and decrease on our own and there are supernatural virtues which have God as their cause.[57] There are the natural virtues of synesis and gnome as well as the supernatural virtues of synesis and gnome. Because supernatural virtues deal with God as their proper object and the

---

[54]Deferrari in *A Latin-English Dictionary of St. Thomas*, p. 443.

[55] ST II-II, q. 51, a. 4.

[56]ST I-II, q. 57, a. 6, ad 3.

[57]For longer discussion of the distinction between these two kinds of virtue, see *Introduction to the Science of Mental Health*, vol. II, chapter 2.

means to God, which includes our salvation, then supernatural prudence which includes supernatural synesis and gnome helps a person to sort out when the common law does not apply in relationship to those matters that touch upon one's salvation or God.

For example, if a Catholic couple took their children to a Mass where the priest after the consecration decided he wanted to have a "dance with Jesus" and took the host and placed it on his head and danced around the sanctuary (which actually happened), even though the Church precept states that we must fulfill our Sunday obligation, if it is the only Mass available, one would not be obligated to take one's children to that Mass. This follows from the fact that the higher principle that one cannot enter heaven without faith supersedes one's obligation to attend Mass; where one's children would be scandalized and their faith affected, one must avoid it. This raises the question: what are the "higher principles" that apply to supernatural synesis and gnome? With natural synesis and gnome, it is the natural law that one reverts to in order to sort out when the common law does not apply. In the case of supernatural synesis and gnome, it is the Divine Positive Law, or one may say divine Revelation, which constitutes the "higher principles." This is why Scripture says, "it is better to obey God than man" [Acts 5:29], even though man at times is endowed with the authority of God.

When the Church enters into a state where a pontiff is saying things contrary to the Faith, as was seen historically with Honorius I or John XXII, one simply cannot follow them because if one were to do so one would end up in heresy. The question then becomes: what must one do in order to avoid ending up in heresy and offending God when not just the pope, but also when a particular bishop says something contrary to the Faith?

Firstly, it must be recognized that even the members of the Magisterium are bound to the **deposit of faith** and the **remote rule of faith**, i.e., that which pertains to the tradition.

Secondly, so are the faithful. In the historical case of John XXII, he did precisely what was supposed to be done. Once it was brought to his attention that he had said something that could be considered erroneous, he consulted the remote rule; the tradition. Subsequent to the findings of the commission that he had established, he then recanted his position. This tells that even the pope and the members of the Magisterium are bound by the tradition of the remote rule and therefore one must go back to the remote rule when one considers what is to be done.

In other words, part of the virtue of prudence which includes gnome is that when something out of the ordinary occurs – a pope or other member of the Magisterium says something contrary to the remote rule – we must consult the remote rule to ensure that our faith is correct. However, there is an entire set of principles which govern how one is to consult the remote rule and how one is to proceed when one finds oneself in that uncommon historical situation;

i.e., in a situation where the pope or other member of the Magisterium says something contrary to the Faith. We must discuss, therefore, the precise nature of those principles.

III: PRINCIPLES OF JUDGMENT

One of the things that we are trying to avoid is becoming Protestants, where one is left to one's own judgment. As a Catholic, in all matters of religion one must submit one's judgment to the judgment of the Church unless the Church in no way has pronounced judgment on the topic. However, once the Church pronounces judgment on it in any way or if there has been a discussion of that topic somewhere in the tradition, we are bound to investigate and submit our judgment to those who are higher than us in the ecclesiastical order. This itself is part of the supernatural virtue of prudence. So even if one finds oneself in a situation where a particular member of the Magisterium is saying things contrary to the Faith, that does not allow us to make our own determination. What we are bound to do is take reasonable means to investigate what the tradition is and conform ourselves to it. That reasonable investigation will involve the following principles.

A. Natural Principles

1. All principles that govern rational thinking must be adhered to in order for a particular teaching of the member of the Magisterium to be held as true. Since truth is one, any contradiction of self- evident metaphysical and logical first principles automatically discredits what any magisterial member says.

For example, the principle of non-contradiction applies even in matters of revelation and theology. That being the case, if one member of the Magisterium contradicts what has been infallibly defined, the very contradiction negates the truth of the statement of the subsequent magisterial member. For instance, if a member of the Magisterium were to say that Christ did not resurrect in the same numerical body as that in which He died, we know this to be directly contrary to Revelation[58] and the constant teaching of the Church. We know, therefore, that what the magisterial member is saying is false.

---

[58] 1Cor. 15:14: "And if Christ be not risen again, then is our preaching vain: and your faith is also vain."

2. The statement is clearly contrary to right reason or the natural law. For example, if one magisterial member were to say that homosexual marriage should be allowed, we know this to be false because marriage by its very nature, according to the natural law, is between one man and one woman. In this case, we would not be permitted to follow that teaching of the magisterial member.

3. The person interpreting the statement made by a member of the Magisterium must (a) have a true grasp of the Church's actual teaching on the matter, and (b) have certitude about what the actual magisterial member said. Precision in knowledge of the Faith is important. All too often people criticise what magisterial member has said when they do not have a proper grasp of what the Church even teaches on the matter. Moreover, given the fact that the media is prone to getting things wrong, one must take pains to ensure that the source from which one is reading or learning is accurate. This is a matter of justice (and charity) to the member of the Magisterium. *prone to having a tendency.*

B. Supernatural Principles

When we shift to the supernatural principles, we recognize that there are a number of them:

1. Any statement that is contrary to the Divine Positive Law, i.e. Revelation, *as the Church has always understood it*, one is bound not to follow

it. This is based on the Vincentian Canon.[59] It is not a matter of what the private individual thinks is contrary to Revelation but what the Church understands to be contrary to Revelation. If any member of the Magisterium teaches something contrary to the Divine Positive Law, one is not permitted to follow that teaching.[60]

2. Based upon the principles governing infallibility, all subsequent popes and members of the Church are bound by the tradition with regard to those things which are infallible. This is obvious from the fact that the teaching is irreformable and incapable of being erroneous. If any member of the Magisterium teaches something contrary to an infallibly proposed teaching, i.e. *de fide* definita or non d*efinita*, one is not permitted to follow that teaching.

3. Popes are also bound by prior non-infallible teachings of the Magisterium which are taught in the tradition, unless they speak with a higher magisterial voice. Essentially what this teaches us is that if a

---

[59]For full discussion of this see this author's work, *The Binding Force of Tradition.*

[60]It should be noted that the following principle applies: abuse does not take away use. If a member of the Magisterium is teaching something contrary to the Faith, we are not permitted to follow his teaching. However, when he does speak as a member of the Magisterium and his teaching is in accordance with the tradition, we are bound to follow him. The tendency to dismiss whatever he may teach due to the one error should be avoided.

number of popes were to teach something in a general audience or the like, then a subsequent pope proposes a teaching in an encyclical, we would be bound by what is in the encyclical and not by what the popes said in their general audiences, since they are of a lower magisterial voice.

4. We are normally bound by non-infallible teachings of the pope and Magisterium. When popes make non-infallible statements, if those statements appear to be erroneous, they must be judged in light of the tradition. This is the gist of what Pope Benedict XVI called the hermeneutic of continuity. It essentially established tradition as the remote rule and the principle of judgment of subsequent magisterial teaching. However, as a matter of warning, one should not simply presume that because the pope is saying something in a non-infallible manner, that one should immediately presume it is erroneous. The benefit of the doubt or the presumption should be that what is being said is true, unless there is clear indication to the contrary.

5. When papal documents or teachings conflict with what curial members or bishops teach, that which is minor gives way to what is major. This is based upon Pope Nicholas I's letter:

> Since, according to the canons, where there is a greater authority, the judgment of the inferiors is to be deferred, viz. to be annulled or to be strengthened: certainly it is evident that the judgment of the Apostolic See, of whose authority there is none greater, is to

be refused by no one. [Denz. 641/333] 和尊

Pope Nicholas then goes on to exhort that one should submit one's judgment to the Church. This principle is fairly simple, e.g. if a bishop were to say something contrary to the pope, one would normally follow the pope.

6. Greater weight is given when more than one pope speaks on an issue than when one pope speaks on an issue, unless the subsequent pope promulgates the teaching infallibly or in a manner which is of higher authority. 权威性

7. If a subsequent teaching does not address a prior teaching, and the prior is more founded on the Deposit of Faith and tradition, one is free to adhere to the prior teaching unless the subsequent teaching is stated in a more authoritative way.

8. In questions of doubt, since even the popes are bound to the tradition as is evidenced by the papal oath, favour in questions of doubt normally falls to tradition. This is based upon the principle that even the popes are bound to the tradition as a matter of precept[61] and subsequent teachings are to be interpreted in light of the tradition.

9. Where two conflicting teachings on non-infallible matters are proposed, the Magisterium has the obligation out of charity, justice and prudence to clarify the teaching and pronounce a judgment. As a matter of prudence, one should

---

[61]This is discussed throughout *The Binding Force of Tradition*.

normally suspend his own personal judgment until the Magisterium has passed judgment on the particular matter. The *final* judgment of the magisterium, particularly the pope or council speaking infallibly, is final.

10. Current disciplinary norms of the current Magisterium bind. This principle would hold true unless there was something contained in the current disciplinary norms that was clearly contrary to the Deposit of Faith or the Church's constant moral teaching.

11. One is never free to make oneself the principle of judgment. This follows from the fact that these are matters of the intellect, not of the will. Therefore, they are matters of judgment, not choice.

12. In matters of doubt where the popes have not clarified or made any determination, or none of the above principles apply, then we follow the principle: in necessary things, unity; in doubtful things, liberty, in all things, charity.[62]

---

[62]In necessariis unitas, in dubiis libertas, in omnibus caritas. This phrase has been attributed to St. Augustine but there is some debate about the attribution.

analyze

IV: THE PROPER RESPONSE TO AN ERRING MAGISTERIAL MEMBER

What does one do if one finds a bishop or even a pope who is saying things contrary to the teaching of the Church as it has always understood it? While the intellectual criteria for what we are to believe is parsed out above, how should we approach the situation spiritually?

The first is to remember that as pope he holds an office which is established by Christ (God) himself and therefore regardless of his teachings, there is always respect and honour due to the office because it is honouring God Himself. Piety is the virtue by which one gives honour to those who are above oneself as well as care of those who are

— *filial piety*
— *to be obedient to one's parents*

consent
reluctantly [Fr. Mr.]
fatally overwhelmed

despite being
although

entrusted to a person.[63] Even if the pope were to
speak error, our attitude of piety should not be
affected or changed. We ought still to show him the
honour that is due to him as our superior. Honour is
the praise or the treatment that we show to
somebody due to some excellence, and the office of
the papacy is an excellence. That means we must
always show the pope honour or reverence as a
matter of showing it to God.   *respect, exalted*

The same principle applies, albeit in a lesser
fashion, even to bishops and priests. While today   *minor*
there might be a number of bishops and priests who
are teaching things contrary to the Faith, it should
not disturb our interior life and it should not affect
our piety towards them. There is great danger in
succumbing to impiety when a person allows one's
interior life to be disturbed by various members of
the magisterium or priests saying things contrary to
the Faith. We should not be disturbed because we see
the same thing playing itself out in scripture, where
Peter denies Christ,[64] or when Peter first holds to the
requirement of circumcision to become a Christian

[63]In ST II-II, q. 101, St. Thomas discusses the fact that
piety deals primarily with God and then our parents and what
he calls "patria"• (those with whom we live in a communal life).
In effect, it is the virtue by which we give honour to those
above us, whether it is God, our parents, or someone else in our
life. See discussion of piety beginning on page 297 in Ripperger,
Introduction to the Science of Mental Health.

[64]Luke 22:54-62; 14:69-70; Matthew 26:73-75; and John
18:13-27.

and later defines the opposite. God is revealing through Revelation itself that these things will occur, and so it is necessary on our part to make sure that we always have the proper spiritual dispositions towards them, so that it does not drag us into error or into lack of virtue.

At times, people will even be scandalised by what the Holy Father says. Scandal is when one allows what another person does to affect one's faith. But as St. Thomas points out, one is never permitted to allow oneself to take scandal because we have an obligation to preserve our faith regardless of what other people do. And this includes everybody from the pope all the way down to the lowest person on the planet.

Again, there we must recognise that these things can happen even though our normal intellectual approach should be to believe what the Magisterium tells us. In that regard, great care must be taken to avoid listening to media outlets which manipulate what the pope and bishops say, in order to place a spin on how people perceive it so as to influence public opinion. As a general rule, given the near complete lack of trustworthiness of the news media, in order to disentangle its spin one should always seek to know what precisely was said by the Holy Father. This itself will help to avoid much confusion and lack of clarity. Moreover, all of those things which are necessary for salvation have already been revealed and taught by the Church. So even if bishops or popes say things contrary to the Faith, we already know what is necessary for

55

salvation. Therefore, nothing should disturb our faith or interior life in this regard.

This brings us to the proper attitude towards any member of the magisterium or clergy and his weakness; we must pray and do penance for him. If we see a bishop say things contrary to our faith, our first approach should not be to criticise him, but to pray and do penance for him. When we stand before God, will we be able adequately to answer the question that Christ may pose to us: "What did you do to help him?" Or "What did you do to help the Church"? If our only reaction is to complain or criticise, our reaction is not out of charity. Charity is the virtue by which we love God and our neighbour for the sake of God. If we love God then we will want his Church to be healthy and we will pray and do penance for it. If we love our neighbour for the sake of God, then we will want him to overcome his error rather than to continue suffering in his error. That requires grace which enlightens the mind and strengthens the will. Therefore, we will pray for him: so that he will receive the illumination in his mind about his error and have the strength of will to accept it. If we do not do that, then we may stand before God for the sin of negligence in relationship to our brother. Many are too quick to break out the billy clubs to beat people over the head rather than to do prayer and penance for them.

There is one last thing that we might consider doing when we see a particular member of the magisterium or clergy say things contrary to the Faith: examine our conscience. We must ask

spiritual awareness.

ourselves the question, "What have I done to deserve better leaders?" We get the leaders we deserve. If we do not have good leaders, i.e. members of the Magisterium deeply committed to an orthodox Catholic faith, what does that say about us as members of the Church? As St. John Eudes says:

The most evident mark of God's anger and the most terrible castigation He can inflict upon the world are manifested when He permits His people to fall into the hands of clergy who are priests more in name than in deed, priests who practice the cruelty of ravening wolves rather than charity and affection of devoted shepherds ... When God permits such things, it is a very positive proof that He is thoroughly angry with His people, and is visiting His most dreadful anger upon them. That is why He cries unceasingly to Christians, "Return o ye revolting children ... and I will give you pastors according to My own heart" (Jer. 3:14,15). Thus, irregularities in the lives of priests constitute a scourge upon the people in consequence of sin.

Let us be clear about one thing: it is not our place to examine the conscience of other people, regardless of how bad a Catholic they may be. When we consider the state of the Church and the fact that many members of the Magisterium and clergy are saying things contrary to the Faith, we should examine our

57

own conscience about any culpability in the matter. We must make sure that our conscience is clear by making sure that we do prayer and penance to make sure that we have priests and bishops who love and teach the orthodox Catholic faith.

Made in the USA
Coppell, TX
23 October 2020